GW00730619

1

LOSING A LEGENDARY ICON
MATTHEW PERRY

Remembering the Iconic Legacy of Matthew Perry, The Inspiring
Life Story of his Early Life, Career, and Humble Beginning.

George Humphrey

TABLE OF CONTENTS

CHAPTER 1: INTRODUCTION

At 54 years old, Matthew Perry, who gained popularity as Chandler Bing on the popular sitcom Friends, passed away.

Perry reportedly drowned to death in his Pacific Palisades, Los Angeles, home, according to law authorities and an agent for the actor.

Friends' ten seasons were produced by Warner Bros. Television Group between 1994 and 2004, and the company paid tribute to *"our dear friend" and "an incredibly gifted actor."*

His humorous brilliance had an international influence, and he will always be remembered in the hearts of countless people. It said, "We send our love to his family, his loved ones, and all of his devoted fans on this heartbreaking day."

Following little appearances in Beverly Hills 90,210, Dream On, and Growing Pains, Perry landed the part of the neurotic and sarcastic Chandler Bing in Friends. With many Emmys and record ratings, the comedy about six friends in New York City swiftly gained popularity. The 2004 conclusion, which attracted over 52 million people in the US, became the most-watched TV program of the 2000s.

"Every day, I get approached by people who say, 'Hey Chandler!'" In an interview from 2014, he stated, "I don't respond to it." Saying hello and expressing admiration for Matthew's work is one thing. But I object if someone says, "Hey, Chandler." I'm over it now. It's not me, Chandler.

Childhood and Youth

On August 19, 1969, Matthew Perry was born in Williamstown, Massachusetts. He was the third child born to actor John Bennett Perry and journalist Suzanne Marie Morrison. Perry spent the majority of his youth living in Ottawa, Ontario, Canada, with his mother and siblings after his parents split when he was a small child.

Perry showed an early interest in performing. He did skits for his family and friends and took part in school performances. Perry traveled to Los Angeles to live with his father and pursue an acting career when he was fifteen years old.

Perry completed his education at Sherman Oaks, California's Buckley School in 1987. Then, to concentrate on his acting career, he dropped out of the University of Southern California after just one year.

Guest roles on TV series like *Second Chance*, *Charles in Charge*, and *Growing Pains* comprised Perry's early acting career. He was cast in an ongoing role on the NBC sitcom *Sydney* in 1989.

Breakthrough Performance in Friends as Chandler Bing

Perry was chosen to star in the NBC sitcom *Friends* as Chandler Bing in 1994. The program was a commercial and critical triumph, establishing Perry as a household figure. From 1994 to 2004, he portrayed Chandler in all 10 of the show's seasons.

Data analyst Chandler Bing is a clever and caustic individual. He is well-known for his love of coffee and his humorous self-deprecation. Chandler Bing, as portrayed by Tyler Perry, is regarded as one of the most recognizable and adored comedy characters ever.

Effects on the Amusement Sector

The entertainment business has greatly benefited from Matthew Perry's contributions. He is among the all-time greatest sitcom performers and is credited with popularizing the "smart aleck" character archetype. Many aspiring performers and comedians have also been inspired by Perry's work on *Friends*.

Apart from his involvement in *Friends*, Perry has acted in several other popular movies and TV series, such as *Almost Heroes* (1998), *Fools Rush In* (1997), *Three to Tango* (1999), *Studio 60 on the Sunset Strip* (2006–2007), and *The Odd Couple* (2015–2017).

Perry is a gifted writer and producer as well. In addition to creating and producing multiple episodes of *Friends*, he has also created and produced several television shows, including *The Odd Couple* and *Studio 60 on the Sunset Strip*.

Perry is a well-known writer, producer, and performer. He continues to inspire and amuse audiences all around the world, leaving a lasting impression on the entertainment sector.

Raising a Family in Massachusetts

Matthew Perry grew up in a lovely Massachusetts childhood. He loved being with his friends and enjoying sports, and he had a great relationship with his mother and siblings.

Perry has stated that his early years in Massachusetts influenced who he is now. Additionally, he has expressed his gratitude for the upbringing he had from his family and friends.

Early Aspirations to Become Actors

Perry showed an early interest in performing. He has stated that the power of narrative and performers' capacity to take viewers to new places has always captivated him.

Perry started acting in school productions at a young age. In addition, he loved to watch television shows and movies, and he would frequently mimic his favorite actors.

Perry claims that even at a very young age, he knew he wanted to be an actor. In addition, he stated that although he knew that pursuing this professional route would be difficult, he was committed to succeeding.

To sum up

Actor, producer, and writer Matthew Perry

enjoys professional success. He continues to inspire and amuse audiences all around the world, leaving a lasting impression on the entertainment sector. Perry's early aspirations to become an actor and his upbringing in Massachusetts influenced both his early life and profession.

CHAPTER 2: CAREER

Television Shows

Matthew Perry has had a successful career in television, appearing in shows such as *Second Chance* (1985), *Charles in Charge* (1985), *Growing Pains* (1987-1989), *Sydney* (1989), *Friends* (1994-2004), *Studio 60 on the Sunset Strip* (2006-2007), *Web Therapy* (2011-2013), *Go On* (2012-2013), *The Good Wife* (2013-2016), *Mr. Sunshine* (2011), *The Odd Couple* (2015-2017), *The Good Fight* (2017) and *Cougar Town* (2014).

His most famous part is that of Chandler Bing from the sitcom *Friends*, which catapulted him to fame both critically and commercially. From 1994 until 2004, Perry portrayed Chandler in all ten of the show's seasons. Chandler Bing is a clever and caustic data analyst who enjoys coffee and has a self-deprecating sense of humor. Chandler Bing, as portrayed by Tyler Perry, is regarded as one of the most recognizable and adored comedy characters ever.

Films

Perry has also starred in several successful films, including *A Night in the Life of Jimmy Reardon* (1988), *Fools Rush In* (1997), *Almost Heroes* (1998), *Three to Tango* (1999), *The Whole Nine Yards* (2000), *Serving Sara* (2002), *The Whole Ten Yards* (2004), *17 Again* (2009), and *Birds of America* (2009).

Video Games

Perry has also provided his voice for video games, including *Fallout: New Vegas* (2010).

Stage Productions

Perry has also appeared in stage productions, including *The End of Longing* (2006).

To sum up

Actor Matthew Perry has enjoyed considerable success during his lengthy career in theater, cinema, video games, and television. His most well-known part is that of Chandler Bing from *Friends*, but he has starred in several other popular shows. Perry is a gifted comedian and actor whose work has delighted viewers all around the world.

Partnerships

Throughout his life, Matthew Perry has been in various relationships. He has dated several well-known celebrities, such as Lizzy Caplan, Yasmine Bleeth, and Julia Roberts. In 2020, Perry was also engaged to literary manager Molly Hurwitz; however, their engagement broke down the following year.

Perry has been transparent about his prior relationship difficulties. He has admitted that his difficulties with substance misuse and his dedication to his work make it difficult for him to stay in committed partnerships over the long run. Perry has, however, also expressed optimism about falling in love in the future.

Drug Abuse and Rehabilitation

For a long time, Matthew Perry has battled substance misuse. He has discussed how his addiction has affected his life and profession and has been candid about his issues.

Perry started using drugs and drinking alcohol at an early age. He claims that he began drinking to help him deal with his social anxieties and blend in with his friends. As Perry grew older, his use of drugs and alcohol increased, and he eventually became severely addicted.

Perry has spent several years in recovery. He has also made multiple relapses. Perry, on the other hand, has been clean for several years.

Perry attributes his success in kicking his addiction to his friends and family. Additionally, he has stated that a major factor in his recuperation has been his faith.

Generosity

Matthew Perry is a philanthropist who donates to many organizations. The National Alliance on Mental Illness (NAMI) has his utmost support. In addition, Perry has made donations to other nonprofit organizations, including Children's Hospital Los Angeles's Matthew Perry Cancer Treatment Center.

Perry has made speeches on the value of giving back to the neighborhood. He has expressed his gratitude for his life's accomplishments and his desire to use his position to assist others.

Individual Challenges and Achievements

In his life, Matthew Perry has surmounted numerous obstacles. He has battled interpersonal issues, mental illness, and substance misuse. Perry, nevertheless, has endured hardships and come out stronger as a result of his perseverance.

Many people find inspiration in Perry. For people who are battling addiction, mental illness, or other personal struggles, he serves as an inspiration. Perry's tale serves as a reminder that even the most formidable obstacles may be surmounted.

Beyond Central Benefits

Popularity stems from Matthew Perry's portrayal of Chandler Bing in the sitcom *Friends*. Perry has, nevertheless, enjoyed a prosperous career outside of Central Perk. acted in several series, movies, and theatrical productions.

Perry is a gifted comedian and actor. He serves as a role model and humanitarian as well. Many individuals find inspiration in Perry, and his narrative serves as a reminder that despite obstacles, it is possible to realize your dreams.

A prosperous actor, philanthropist, and role model is Matthew Perry. He has surmounted numerous obstacles in his life and come out stronger as a result. Many individuals find inspiration in Perry, and his narrative serves as a reminder that despite obstacles, it is possible to realize your dreams.

CHAPTER 4: BATTLES AND RESILIENCE

It was not an easy road for Matthew Perry to become a sober advocate for mental health. For many years, he battled alcohol and prescription medication addiction, which affected his mental health. But he overcame his obstacles and emerged as a formidable champion for others thanks to his tenacity and fortitude.

When Perry was in his early twenties, his addiction started. He began taking Vicodin to treat his back pain, but the drug gradually created a dependency on him. In addition, he started drinking excessively, and his drug usage got out of hand.

Perry's personal and professional lives were severely impacted by his addiction. He had to take many interruptions from filming Friends due to drug and alcohol-related issues, which landed him in the hospital multiple times. Because of his addiction, he also lost several instances and relationships.

Perry eventually struck rock bottom in 1997. After ingesting 28 Vicodin tablets and drinking vodka, he was admitted to the hospital. He eventually realized that he required assistance after that occurrence. He entered treatment, starting the protracted and challenging process of becoming well.

Perry's recuperation wasn't always simple. Over the years, he experienced multiple relapses, but he never gave up. He persisted in attending therapy sessions and working on maintaining sobriety, ultimately leading to a sustained recovery.

Perry decided to use his position to support people dealing with addiction and mental health problems when he got sober. He started speaking out in favor of mental health awareness and rehabilitation. He has been transparent about his objectives and encouraged a lot of others to ask for assistance.

In Malibu, California, Perry established the Perry House, a sober living facility for men, in 2013. For males in recovery from addiction, The Perry House offers a secure and encouraging setting. Perry is also active with several other charities that support addiction and mental health.

Perry's tale is one of resiliency and optimism. He overcame great obstacles to become sober and a well-known mental health advocate. Many people who are battling addiction and mental health concerns find encouragement in him.

The following are particular instances of Perry's support for mental health:

* Perry discussed the value of mental health treatment in testimony given in 2015 before the US Senate Committee on Health, Education, Labor, and Pensions. Perry established the Matthew Perry Foundation in 2016 to fund mental health research and services. * In his memoir "Friends, Lovers, and the Big Terrible Thing," published in 2017, Perry openly talked about his battles with drugs and mental illness. Perry also frequently speaks at conferences and gatherings on addiction and mental health.

Many individuals have been motivated to seek assistance by Perry's advocacy, which has contributed to an increase in awareness of addiction and mental illness. He truly serves as an inspiration to those who are facing similar difficulties.

CHAPTER 5: HOLLYWOOD SUCCESS AND SETBACKS

The Hollywood career of Matthew Perry has been characterized by both achievements and disappointments. He has overcome tremendous obstacles in addition to reaching amazing heights. He has persevered in being faithful to his trade and producing excellent work despite the ups and downs.

Without question, Perry's most famous part was that of Chandler Bing in the comedy Friends. The program became a worldwide sensation and established Perry as a household figure. His comedic timing and ability to make Chandler come to life won him accolades.

In addition, Perry starred in several movies, such as 17 Again, Almost Heroes, Fools Rush In, and The Whole Nine Yards. In addition, he starred in several television programs, such as Mr. Sunshine and Studio 60 on the Sunset Strip.

Perry's success did not, however, come without difficulties. He battled mental illness and addiction for a long time, and these problems frequently affected his ability to do his job. In the early 2000s, he too experienced a run of box office failures.

Perry has maintained a constant work schedule throughout his career despite the setbacks. He has consistently demonstrated a great deal of fortitude and tenacity, and he has never given up on his goal of becoming a well-known actor.

Here are some particular instances of Perry's successes and difficulties:

Results attained:

*Won a Screen Actors Guild Award for Outstanding Performance by an Ensemble in a Comedy Series for his work on Friends * Nominated for seven Primetime Emmy Awards for Outstanding Supporting Actor in a Comedy Series for his role as Chandler Bing on Friends * Starred in several popular films, including Fools Rush In, Almost Heroes, The Whole Nine Yards, and 17 Again

* Established the Matthew Perry Foundation, which offers money for mental health research and treatment; * Founded the Perry House, a sober living facility for men in Malibu, California; authored a memoir titled "Friends, Lovers, and the Big Terrible Thing," in which he openly talked about his battles with mental illness and addiction.

Difficulties:

* Fought for many years with alcohol and prescription drug addiction; * Several times had to take breaks from filming Friends

because of his addiction; Due to his addiction, he lost several acquaintances and relationships. had a run of financially disastrous films in the early 2000s.

Perry has consistently stayed loyal to his art despite the difficulties. He is a gifted comedian and actor who is enthusiastic about what he does. He serves as an inspiration to people who are battling addiction and mental health problems.

Remaining Accurate in His Craft

Perry has always had a strong dedication to his work. He takes great pride in his job and is a perfectionist. He is renowned for being kind and eager to support other performers.

Perry has stated that he believes he must change the world with his platform. His goal is to support people who are battling mental illness and addiction. In addition, he hopes to encourage others to pursue their goals despite difficulties.

Perry is a real-life success story in Hollywood. He overcame great obstacles to realize his goals. Many people look up to him, and he will undoubtedly continue to produce excellent work for many years to come.

Influence on Culture at Large

There is no denying Matthew Perry's influence on popular culture. One of the most recognizable and adored sitcom characters of all time is him from his role as Chandler Bing on Friends. Because of his sardonic wit and dry humor, Chandler is still a well-liked figure among audiences of all ages.

In addition, Perry's work on Friends influenced how young people were portrayed in popular culture. Among the first television series to portray young adults in their twenties and thirties accurately was Friends. The program tackled topics including friendships, careers, and relationships in a lighthearted and realistic manner.

In addition, Perry's work on Friends contributed to the spread of the idea of the "sitcom gang." One of the first television series to highlight a close-knit group of friends who helped one another through good times and bad was Friends. This idea has since been carried out in numerous other sitcoms, which is evidence of Friends' ongoing appeal.

Motivation for Others

Others can find inspiration in Perry's tale as well. To fulfill his objectives, he has surmounted enormous obstacles like addiction and mental illness. He serves as an inspiration to those who are facing similar difficulties by demonstrating that achievement is achievable even in the face of adversity.

Comedians and actresses find inspiration in Perry as well. He has a wonderful sense of comedic timing and is a gifted performer. In addition, he is a workaholic who is quite proud of his accomplishments. For aspiring comedians and actors in the entertainment business, he serves as an inspiration.

ties with the cast of "Friends"

Perry remained connected to his Friends cast members even after the show's 2004 cancellation. He's stated that he views his fellow cast members as his family.

Perry has received support from the Friends cast during his battles with addiction and mental illness. They have supported him throughout his recuperation and urged him to get assistance.

Perry's tight relationship with his Friends co-stars is evidence of the solid bonds that were created on the show. Even now, the cast members remain close friends who stick by one another through good times and bad.

Matthew Perry leaves behind a history of achievement, tenacity, and motivation. He has delighted audiences for decades as a gifted comic and actor. In addition, he serves as an inspiration for those who are battling mental illness and addiction. Perry has had an indisputable influence on popular culture, and he will always be regarded as one of the most recognizable sitcom characters ever.

For many years, audiences were delighted by the superb acting and comedic skills of Matthew Perry. He served as an inspiration to many battling mental illness and addiction. Perry has had an indisputable influence on popular culture, and he will always be regarded as one of the most recognizable sitcom characters ever.

Appendix

List of Film Credits

* Fools Rush In ([1997](#))
* Almost Heroes ([1998](#))
* Three to Tango ([1999](#))
* The Whole Nine Yards ([2000](#))
* Serving Sara ([2002](#))
* The Whole Ten Yards ([2004](#))
* Numb ([2007](#))
* 17 Again ([2009](#))

* The Odd Couple ([2016](#))

List of Television Credits

* Boys Will Be Boys ([1987](#))
* Charles in Charge ([1987–1988](#))
* A Night in the Life of Jimmy Reardon ([1988](#))
* She's Out of Control ([1989–1990](#))
* L.A. Law ([1990](#))
* Sydney ([1992](#))
* Home Free ([1993](#))
* Friends ([1994–2004](#))
* Studio 60 on the Sunset Strip ([2006–2007](#))
* Mr. Sunshine ([2011](#))
* Go On ([2012–2013](#))
* The Odd Couple ([2015–2017](#))

List of Video Game Credits

Fallout: New Vegas ([2010](#))

List of Stage Productions Credits

* The Speed of Darkness (1995)
* Sexual Perversity in Chicago (1997)
* When Harry Met Sally... (2004)
* The End of Steve (2006)
* The Odd Couple (2013)

A variety of comedies, dramas, and romantic comedies can be found throughout Perry's filmography. He has starred in several popular movies and TV series, but his most well-known role is that of Chandler Bing from the comedy Friends. Perry's acting ability is demonstrated by the variety of roles he has taken on.

Printed in Great Britain
by Amazon

37270284R00020